INSTRUCTIONS FOR
THE PROPER CREMATION
OF YOUR GRIEF

Amber Decker

FOLKWAYS PRESS, LLC

Texas, USA
www.folkwayspress.com

Instructions For the Proper Cremation of Your Grief
first published in 2022

Text © Amber Decker, 2022

Cover design by Amanda Hooser

ISBN: 978-1-7362701-2-7

All rights reserved. This publication may not
be reproduced, stored in a retrieval system or
transmitted, in any form or by any means – electronic,
mechanical, photocopying, recording or otherwise,
without the prior permission of the publisher

CONTENTS

This Is the Story	3
Less Than	6
The Magic and the Moon	9
On A Good Day I Will Tell You It Was Rape	12
Coal Miner's Daughter	15
The Slender Man	18
Late to the Party, but This Party Is Mine	22
When He Says, "You Looked So Beautiful in That Dress"	25
Repeat	29
"Surplus Killing"	31
The Dust and the Ashes	34
Telling the Bees	38
Instructions for the Proper Cremation of Your Grief	40
I've Never Trusted Hollywood	43
The Not-Leaving	46
Elegy	49
I Love You Like a Wounded Creature	52

INSTRUCTIONS FOR
THE PROPER CREMATION
OF YOUR GRIEF

THIS IS THE
STORY

in which i never wed
in which i spend my life in a tower
smoothing my hair into braids

in which i am really a boy
who has a sister
who doesn't speak

in which my sister curls herself
against me at night in bed like a cursive 'C'

in which my sister covers
her pretty face with her hands

in which i am really a killer
in a gingerbread house

AMBER DECKER

in which even my death
at the hands of the hero
is delicious

in which i am really a sorceress
able to disarm whatever lock
skin can fashion itself into

in which i am fallow
and beautiful
and wasp-waisted
and sweet
and starving

in which i prick my finger
just so I can finally get some sleep

in which i am wine
in a silver goblet,
the poisoned apple
in the witch's basket

THIS IS THE STORY

in which i am the secret princess
whose throat shivers
under the blade of the huntsman's knife
as she begs for her life

in which i am the queen
devouring the throat of the man
who offered me a pig's heart
in place of what i asked for

in which i am the pig
in which i am the heart
plunged into the iron pot

LESS THAN

After my mother cut my hair too short one night,
an older girl on the school bus
the next morning asked me mockingly
if I was a boy, and I could only
shake my head
and look at the raised half-moon of a scab
on my knee.

Later, a male teacher told me
I needed to start wearing a bra,
my white t-shirt transformed
into idle distraction by my budding
adolescent chest.
I shrugged my shoulders together,
sank further down in my seat.

For years, I was never quite sure
what was expected from me.

LESS THAN

When I wore dresses, boys tried
to put their hands under my skirt.
My father looked away when I undressed.
My mother furiously washed the blush
from my face
with a wet napkin.
Friends told me I was too pale.
I needed to spend more time in the sun,

to be less abrasive,
less angry,
less emotional,
less selfish,
less quiet,
less shy
less bossy,
always less of something,

and to keep smiling
no matter what.

AMBER DECKER

At bath time, I lined up
my Barbies on the rim of the tub.
I turned the water on as hot as it could go,
held the heads of my dolls under the spray
until my own real skin
was red with heat. I could never burn
the bliss from their faces,
wash the lipstick smiles
from their mouths. They never complained –
just waited ever-patient in their vinyl cases until
I brought them out into the light long enough
to brush their hair until their grinning heads
popped off
in my chubby, nail-bitten hands,
until the little pink comb
was full of the unbothered, blonde pieces of them.

THE MAGIC AND
THE MOON

I asked if you believed in Bigfoot,
and you said yes without hesitation.
You lusted openly after countless unknowns
hidden away like a gallery of freaks
under the striped hood of a circus tent.
You said you wanted to fly to Scotland,
to take a boat out to the center of Loch Ness
in the wee hours, hoping for a glimpse
of long, scaled neck glimmering under stars,
but taking such a long vacation
was not practical, and you were sure your boss
would resent you.
You liked the idea of hunting for monsters
in the dead of night, of capturing a beast
that would make you famous and wearing
its bones around your neck for good luck.

AMBER DECKER

I was a she-wolf whose appetite
might shift with shape of the moon.
You wanted to put a ring on my finger;
you wanted promises, and monogamy,
and morning coffee
and for the train that carried you to and from work
to always be on time, and home-cooked meals,
and a bed made up with hospital corners,
and perfectly folded towels,
and red lips that never smeared
to kiss you goodnight, and children
that sold lemonade on a manicured
front lawn and caught
lightning bugs in mason jars
and never talked back.
From you, I learned there is nothing
humanity cannot drain the magic
and the moon right out of.
At the convenience store, you bought
me black coffee, chocolate, and (thankfully) tampons.
We stood in the parking lot
to smoke and watched snow flurries

THE MAGIC AND THE MOON

dust the footsteps of strangers
who hurried off into the night
with their gas receipts, their cases of beer,
headlights flaring to life like torches
as they pulled out onto the dark road.
I must have looked like such a sad girl
with my messy hair,
curls stuck to the pink gloss on my lips,
my too-white face and ripped black tights.
At twenty-two, I was a mystery even to myself,
and I never expected you to understand me.
You wanted something to chase, something
to lure out into the sunlight
so you could put it into a cage and
put it on display with your name up in lights.
All I wanted was for someone to know
how I've always loved to dance,
even when there is no music,
and especially when no one is watching.

ON A GOOD DAY
I WILL TELL YOU IT
WAS RAPE

Something I never asked for,
and every second of it hurt.
It was February; there was snow on the ground.
Everything was still, including my heartbeat
for a solid seventeen seconds.
There was blood. I floated over our bodies
and saw myself frozen
as Snow White in her glass coffin.
Every word I have ever known
stuck in my throat like jagged slivers
of apple flesh.
I thought I was dead then.
Sometimes, I still do.

ON A GOOD DAY I WILL TELL YOU IT WAS RAPE

My neighbor goes hunting each year.
He hangs deer by their hind legs
from the big tree in his yard
so they can bleed out.
The crows come to poke at the corpses
with beaks sharp as carving knives.
He chases them off, but they always come back,
shiny black wings caked
with blood. They cackle long
into the evening; they love
the game and the small bones
they come away with like trophies.

On a bad day, I will tell you
that some dark siren inside of me stirred
whatever beast dwelled
in the cage of his ribs.
And when my heart went silent,
it slumbered inside of me
with a full stomach.
I will talk about how his eyes
went black as the sun

with the spent body of the moon
draped over it.
I will talk about need, and what it is
to be empty as a patch of ground
waiting to be filled
with the seed
of whatever flesh it can find.

When I was a child, someone cruel
once told me that biting my fingernails
would cause a cancer that would eat
through me like hot piss eats through snow.
I think of it now years later,
and cannot help
but continue sinking my teeth
into the thing I love, again and again,
until something unkillable takes root inside,
until what is left of me must be cut away
without mercy.

COAL MINER'S DAUGHTER

I am a lover of all the dark places
the headlights of my car can never touch.
My empty womb is jealous
of the warm orchards
where the black-eyed children
of Appalachia gather at night
to pick apples
with their skeletal fingers
by the light of the moon.
Hello mountain full of stories.
Hello road full of dead men's curves.
Hello dear ghosts,
dear cauldron,
dear witches in a haze
of purple smoke
and a flash of fire.

AMBER DECKER

Hello vultures happy
and warm in the flesh
of the freshly-killed.
Hello whiskey
down the red tunnel
of my throat,
legs tangled in white sheets.
Hello strangers I have loved
in the tall grass of the holler,
in the backseats of hot cars,
in sleeping bags
down by the whispering river
where the tree frogs sing.
Hello rear view mirror
torn off in the fury of everything dead
inside of me.
I curse you out
like a spot of blood
on the carpet.
I'll put away the knife.
I'll drink the wine.
I'll remember

COAL MINER'S DAUGHTER

what you taught me
before the oaks were tall enough
to cast shadows across
the folded treasure map of your face,
across the crooked gravestones
of every small-town churchyard.

THE SLENDER
MAN

It is the childhood playground,
among the sad, abandoned swingset
and the decomposing metal skeletons of farm animals,
their feet made of springs sunk like thirsty roots
deep into the earth. This is where he came to you
first, in the waning light, the long purple wings of dusk
folded against the peaked roof of the strip mall
across the road.

The man with no face scared you less than the others –

the three older boys who followed you into the woods
as you walked home from school, how their footsteps
quickened when yours did, how they laughed
and called out,

THE SLENDER MAN

"Hey! Slow down, honey!
We just want to talk
to you."

There was a rumble, a sound like a heavy cathedral door
sliding over stone, and they were gone.
Not simply disappeared. Dissolved. Dissolved into
    nothing,
voices fading out of existence like the fizz
of a fountain soda dissipating in summer air.

You imagined a velvet bag drawn closed,
tucked into a hidden pocket
inside a black suit.

There was the man who swung open
the passenger door of his blue car
at a red light while you straddled your bike at the curb,
denim shorts tight on widening hips
as you leaned into a 90-degree August heat.

AMBER DECKER

He rubbed his crotch, said,
"Come here, baby. I got something
to show you."

And all you can recall is dropping your bike
onto the pavement and sprinting
into an alley. Then the crash, the shattering
of glass like raindrops
on a tin roof, the wail of an ambulance,
a woman crying, then silence.

Sometimes, he would leave notes
tucked into the slats of a park bench.
Black hearts scribbled in pen,
markings that reminded you of snow on a
   television screen.
Stick figures of men with
X's through their thin little bird chests.

He was always hungriest in the winter,
when the long nights became a wet mouth
you were happy to languish in for hours
knowing that no one could touch you.

THE SLENDER MAN

You think of the last man who lured you
onto a lonely road, unfastened you
on a snowy hillside and greedily drank in
like a sweet wine what you never offered.
You remember the taste of his ribs
hard as a diamond ring
between your teeth,

but little else.

The wind picks up, and you watch a playground
    swing
stir as the streetlights flicker on
and begin to buzz.
When the rain comes, it puddles at your feet
like a wedding gown;
it walks you home
in ravenous shoes.

LATE TO THE PARTY, BUT THIS PARTY IS MINE

My heart is a room full of red balloons,
dimly lit, heated by naked bodies
and winter kindling. A bear-skin rug.
A January birthday.
The crackle of a record spinning
in the dark, the skip
of the needle.
Men like you are bulls
charging, smashing all the plates
before anyone gets to the cake.
The promise that a boy named Johnny
will always make Leslie Gore cry,
because juke boxes exist
and quarters fall from rips in pockets,
shimmy into the grout of bathroom tiles
to be scooped up,

LATE TO THE PARTY, BUT THIS PARTY IS MINE

recycled in well-meaning fits
of loneliness.
Otis Redding is always Otis Redding.
John Coltrane is always John Coltrane.
Hendrix is always goddamn.
A diamond ring lost
on the floorboard of a little red corvette
parked in the last row at a drive-in movie.
The creature rising from the lagoon,
with eyes like twin black holes
that swallow up all the stars.
A killer who knows the streets
of his city, the swan-like necks of its women
as intimately as he knows
the blue tributaries of his own veins
under his white, white skin.
Yesterday, I dreamt I ran
through forests and graveyards
to get away from you. But the doors
were all locked, and the keys never fit,
and no one was home.

AMBER DECKER

Tonight, the river lullabies its dead
to sleep while you smoke
your cheap cigarettes in the rain
and wait for me to get off work,
to step into the cold rain.
This is where the fairytale ends
like a broken fire escape ladder
dropping down into the alleyway below.
Tonight, the wolf is in bed with the girl, gobbling.
Fine. Tonight, I feel strong enough
to be the axe raised like a beacon.
Look at all those guts spilling out
like crackerjacks
across the tiled kitchen floor.
The black stones, the red stitches
knotted up like ribbons,
like wet roses on a grave.

WHEN HE SAYS
"YOU LOOKED SO BEAUTIFUL
IN THAT BLUE DRESS"

Or, "You wore a white flower in your hair,"
I am flabbergasted.

I am always surprised when anyone remembers
anything about me, even if it's just my face
in a crowd of people whose voices
are always louder than mine, whose words are like elegant,
long-limbed women in tailored gowns
descending staircases and never trip
over the red rug of the tongue on the way out.

There are so many beautiful women
in the world, and I have never
felt like one of them.

AMBER DECKER

There are not enough words
in any language to explain why seeing Orion
burning like a torch in the winter sky
balls my heart into an icy fist,
or why a herd of deer in a field
with the setting sun glancing off their softness
makes me weep, or why
I can't drink Irish coffee
without imagining his naked back
in the shower.

I could say,
we made love on his porch
in the middle of the night
with the cold rain falling
all around us.
I could say,
he made coffee.
I could say,
he held me when I wanted to die
and quietly said, "I love you,"
when he thought I was asleep.

WHEN HE SAYS "YOU LOOKED SO BEAUTIFUL..."

The story of our skin
woven together
is rooted like a bright ruby
in my sacrum,

and when it makes me crazy,
there is no map to show me
where to go or not, nothing
to stick a pin into.

What memory of me
will be left to hitch his breath
when there is no body
blushing under his hands?
When I have returned to nothing
but dust and stars?

Maybe it's enough to hope
that when he is left with only
my scent on his pillow
and pieces of my hair curled

around the teeth of his black comb,
he will pause whenever he sees
a woman in a blue dress, even if
it is only long enough to look
for the flower in her hair.

REPEAT

My parents took me out for pizza
every Saturday night to a hole-in-the-wall joint
with red booths that curved like question marks
and a dimly lit back room with a Dungeons & Dragons
pinball machine and a jukebox. I begged my dad
    for quarters
so I could play Carly Simon's
"You're So Vain" over and over.
I wanted a voice like hers, like smoky velvet,
and her long, straight curtain of hair
but at nine, I settled for the feeling of imagined control
I found as the shiny metal arm of the jukebox
skimmed over the neat stack of 45s, and slipped
the record I wanted under the needle
again and again.
This is the image I come back to in my head
each time your number lights up the screen of my
    cell phone

in the dark and I choose to answer
like a well-oiled machine.
You are the child with a pocket full of quarters
and nothing better to do on a Saturday night.
You are the arm and the needle.
I am the song captured under glass,
repeating, repeating lines like
"You gave away the things you loved
and one of them was me."

"SURPLUS KILLING"

In Wyoming, a pack of wolves slaughter
19 elks over the course of a single night,
leave the ripped bodies to rot
in the daylight on the morning
I pull my rental into a tiny gas station
in Sweetwater County to fill up
and grab a cup of terrible coffee.
It is 10 am, and the rough, red faces
of the men here terrify me
as a few offer to pump my gas
or check my oil.
I can't stop thinking about wolves,
about the shadows that have been nipping
at my heels, chasing me down
interstates late at night while the moon
gorges itself on the cold mountain light.
The bruises on my wrists
are silent under the sleeves of my jacket.

AMBER DECKER

Every song on the radio
sounds like obsession, and I
can no longer form the words to sing along.
I stop to eat breakfast at a small
roadside diner where the waitress
brings me a plate of runny eggs and limp bacon.
A man sitting on a stool at the counter
spins around and snaps my bra strap
with a smirk when I get up to use the restroom.
His buddies laugh, and
I feel the black lace break apart
as if it is the only thing holding me together.
To save some money, I consider
spending the night at a rest stop,
but the ghosts of the women
whose bodies have
never been found
tell me I deserve to be more
than some blood spattered
against the snow-covered hillside,
a black boot tossed into a ditch.

"SURPLUS KILLING"

The rest of my coffee goes down cold
and feels like the body of the moon
caught in my throat.
My phone's weather app tells me it is 14 degrees;
something else tells me you better
keep running if you're going to make it
through the night.

THE DUST
AND THE ASHES

This kind of night is too quiet;
the rain falls in sheets,
and makes the unlined road look
like a pane of glass.
I bought my mother a green rain jacket
for her birthday
in June. She only
got to wear it once;
that makes me sad
as the dust on her kitchen table,
and the black Bible
no human hand has touched
in months.
I can't make myself
take out the trash.

THE DUST AND THE ASHES

I count cans of tomatoes,
of sweet peas,
of yellow corn,
like I count cows on a hill
in a field
on a rainy day.
My mother's ashes look tired
in their black box
on the mantle.
I break down in tears
at the grocery store,
a box of unfrosted
strawberry Pop-Tarts
in my hand. My mother had
craved these, and I had forgotten
she would no longer be hungry
or thirsty
or cold.
I pull up the hood
of my red jacket, step
into the rain
like stepping out

of my mother's wardrobe
as a child, hoping to see a lamppost
in the snow – a white queen
offering sweets, telling me
I am pretty.
My mother was the prettiest woman
I ever knew. Even with
a chemo needle in her chest.
Even with her missing breast.
Even with her mismatched socks
full of holes,
her crooked teeth,
her gray hair, crone face.
Even soaked down to the bones
after hiking miles through the rain
because it was a beautiful day,
and we laughed
as we stole peaches
from a neighbor's tree, washed
them in the creek, sated
our hunger for one final
taste of what was left of summer.

THE DUST AND THE ASHES

Sometimes, I eat and taste
ashes
when I swallow.
With a finger, I write
I AM STILL HERE
beside my mother's Bible
in the dust,
because sometimes
I forget.

TELLING THE BEES

Someone has to do the thing,
to say the words aloud
to the hive in the eaves –
"The lady of the house has died."

This house has become
an empty, withered flower
at the mercy of every storm
that threatens to darken the sky,
to break stems in its hard grasp.

As girls, we blew dandelion seeds
into the wind
and set our wishes free
under summer clouds.

Who can say
what is planted?

TELLING THE BEES

What is eaten,
or harvested,
or drowned in puddles?
Everything is a circle
of fire within
a circle of fire.

The dry earth holds our bones
inside of it like a mother
who keeps baby teeth
secreted away in her sewing drawer.

She has to remind herself
that we were small once,
and all of us could fit safely
inside the circle of her arms.

INSTRUCTIONS FOR
THE PROPER CREMATION
OF YOUR GRIEF

The guidebooks all say keep out
of the underground
where everything has been on fire
for years.

The tunnels are collapsed throats
where nothing can breathe,
and you know all of this,
but you like the taste
of oblivion once in awhile –
the corpse pose.

The white gown gone
to ash, to graveyard soil.

INSTRUCTIONS

Throw in the gun he placed to your temple,
the dead dog wrapped up
like a sleepy toddler
in her purple blanket,

the sharp, hinged wrist bones
of winter. Let go of the angry,
the sad, the empty churches
where your red lips
would have seen you crucified,

the empty stomach you
thought would sculpt you
into a nymph of desire.

Build a casket for the sweet line
of his jaw, his kiss,
his scent, the taste of his cock
in your mouth, the cigarette butts
abandoned along the hilly path.

AMBER DECKER

Look at how the sun
sinks like a black boat
between the mountains, how
it paints the snow with flame,

how it ferries you like a frozen queen
to the other side of daylight
silent as every death you've escaped
on little cat feet,

how you are still the child
playing with the red fire truck
in the upstairs hall
of the burning house,

grasping rungs of smoke
on your way down.

I'VE NEVER TRUSTED
HOLLYWOOD

When I squealed at the sight
of the powder blue Cadillac
on the rental lot, you asked the lady
behind the counter how much
and didn't flinch when she quoted a number
that made me feel uneasy,
like you might think I'd owe you
more than a hand to hold, more than
a cup of coffee, or a plate of eggs
in the morning. We bought
one of those stupid tourist maps
of the Hollywood Hills that has little stars
next to the homes of famous people.
You told me your grandmother used to party
with Bela Lugosi, and I believed you.

AMBER DECKER

We passed by his sprawling, gated mansion,
and I felt something cold tickle the back
of my neck. I thought of Jayne Mansfield
and wondered if she'd had time
to feel her head leaving
the rest of her well-shaped body behind, or
if she was already dead before that.
You pressed me against the car's
beige leather interior
and kissed the pulse in my throat,
sucked at it until I felt all my blood rush
to the surface. You were as charming as a young
Count Dracula, and that night I found myself unable
to sleep and wandering
the long, desolate halls of our old hotel
like Mina in her white nightgown
with her mind half-rotted.
Outside in the garden,
a man in a black coat
at an umbrellaed table
offered to cut me a line of coke.

I'VE NEVER TRUSTED HOLLYWOOD

I ignored him and busied myself with the flowers,
bowing to press my nose into the white blossoms
still spread wide open
under the hazy July moon,
happily eating all the light they could gather.
A dog barked in the distance;
several dogs answered back.
Possibly a warning.
But the man had gone, and taken his drugs
with him, and for a moment
I mourned his loss.
From where I knelt, I could see
the powder blue Cadillac
parked under a streetlamp, resting
like a restless animal.
There have been so many times
I have decided to be dangerous
long after the danger has passed.

THE NOT-LEAVING

He says he locked eyes
with the brown-eyed girl in the yellow tank top
in a hut in the humid center
of the Amazon Rainforest,
and that was all it took for the continent
of his heart to shift, to crack into two jagged pieces.
Together, they drank the offered cups of Ayahuasca.
He held back her hair as she wretched.
She dabbed the beads of sweat from his forehead.
They held hands as the trees turned purple and melted
into the shapes of animals with human faces.
How easy is it to lose a wedding ring
in the mud, among the wet and the chirping of frogs?
But love does not always equal staying.
Even stars become sad and tired,
surrender to the charms of the darkness,
extinguish.

THE NOT-LEAVING

It's difficult for me to think of all of this
without thinking of us. I remember
you saying you should have left me alone.
I swallowed lies like a fistful of pills;
I guided the needle into my own vein.
I saw stars. I saw God.
In a dream, I saw deer next to the river
with their heads bowed in sadness.
Today, over a cup of coffee at a tiny cafe,
my new friend tells me he went home to his wife
as if nothing had happened.
There is not a day, he says, when she kisses him,
when she presses her small body against his
with the hunger of a thing not loved
in the way that it deserves to be,
that he does not regret the not-leaving,
the not-knowing who he could have been
with the right woman.
Sometimes he sees
a brown-haired girl in a yellow tank top
and wonders who is kissing her

when the sun goes down
and the sounds of animals screaming their honest love
into the summer heat
keep him awake at night.

ELEGY

I can see grief knocking
at the doorways of my eyes,
the green irises a swirling nightmare
of mourn, but not sleep. Never sleep.
My bones are busy
trying to climb out of my skin,
to shed what no longer serves them.
My soul longs to return to stars,
to the lap of the blessed virgin,
to the black void, wherever you are.
I am no longer sure what to believe.
I used to be so sure
of everything:
The white house, the dog in the yard,
the black mailbox full of bills
for all the physical things we once wanted
so desperately but couldn't

really afford. Now all I want
is to touch what is
no longer alive.
I draw a bath. I sink into and under the water.
I rub my skin raw and never feel clean enough.
There is no longer peace in the trees
or the storms,
the sizzle of summer sidewalk,
the sun's hot hands on my shoulders
while I kneel in the garden
coaxing the seeds of what I hope will be
soft blue flowers into the dirt.
I want to bury myself up to my neck
and let the animals have what is left –
beautiful meat.
I want to be the ghost in the bathroom mirror
of this old house someday.
I will allow some future child,
unable to sleep, to grant me a new name,
to pull me back from the other side,
a Bloody Mary unearthed

ELEGY

like the bones of a murder victim
after the rains come.
I imagine walking to my car at night,
being caught by the throat.
To disappear like this is effortless.
It requires only to be a woman
with a body, without
your body.

I LOVE YOU LIKE A WOUNDED CREATURE

Each morning I wake
from a dream that you have left me,
and my body feels so hopeless and cold
as though my heart hangs from a meat hook
in the dark.
No one ever thinks of loss
until it has opened its giant wings and cast
a long shadow across the smooth body
of one's life.
I was born with a wad of black cloth stuffed
inside my mouth.
I never expected my father to wither
like a houseplant, like a diseased cat.
Now my hands are always cold, and I don't
know how to fix anything.

I LOVE YOU LIKE A WOUNDED CREATURE

I shatter mirrors
and lightbulbs. I've never changed a tire.
I used to want to break the neck
of every soft, living thing.
I hated the way animals
would rub their bodies
against me, blindly loving every
ugly thing I held under my skin.
Given time, everything will rot away
or wander off, and I worry
there is never enough love
to stop it.
Each morning, you bring me coffee
in bed, and I am sad
because I know when you are gone
I will miss these small moments
full of sun and birdsong,
the heat of the green mug
pressed between my palms.
But you smile
and kiss my forehead,

AMBER DECKER

tell me I am always beautiful
even on days when I feel
shipwrecked by whatever injuries
I have gathered to me
in dreams,
sewn like spider's webs
into my palms.
And you stay.
You stay.
You stay.

ABOUT THE AUTHOR

Amber Decker is an Elder Millennial who has loved poetry, mythology, magic, and fairytales her whole life. She has performed her poems across the United States, from her home state of West Virginia to the California coast. Amber has degrees in English and history, but ultimately chose to dedicate herself to practicing massage therapy; she lives happily in Appalachia with her husband and their German shepherd, Max.

www.ingramcontent.com/pod-product-compliance
Lightning Source LLC
Chambersburg PA
CBHW030311100526
44590CB00012B/601